David and Allison
for your family!

Easter Apr '04
We love you so very Much!
Love
moms Dad Nugent

Faith is coming to earth when your true home is heaven.

Hope is living happily, even though you sometimes get hungry, wet, cold, and sad.

And *charity* is the calm assurance that heaven is only a prayer away.

❦

And now abideth faith, hope, charity, these three;
but the greatest of these is charity.
—1 Corinthians 13:13

For Lloyd
—KHN

To my mother, Myrtle Joy Wadsworth Free, my family, and the
wonderful children who inspired these paintings
—MAFS

Text © 2003 Karmel H. Newell
Illustrations © 2003 MaryAnn Free Smith

Visit us at deseretbook.com

Library of Congress Cataloging-in-Publication Data

Newell, Karmel H.
    Come follow me : a child's guide to faith, hope, and charity / written by Karmel H. Newell ; illustrated by MaryAnn Free Smith.
        p.   cm.
    Summary: Explains the biblical concepts of faith, hope, and charity by exploring such things as friendship, participation in church, confronting the death of a grandparent, and seeking forgiveness.
    ISBN 1-57008-809-8
    1. Theological virtues—Juvenile literature.   2. Mormon children—Religious life—Juvenile literature.   [1. Virtues.   2. Mormons—Religious life.
    3. Christian life.]   I. Smith, MaryAnn Free, ill.   II. Title.
    BV4635.N47   2003
    248.8'2—dc21
    [B]   2002153745

Printed in China   68875-6941

Palace Press International, Hong Kong

10   9   8   7   6   5   4   3   2   1

COME, FOLLOW ME

A Child's Guide to Faith, Hope, and Charity

WRITTEN BY KARMEL H. NEWELL
ILLUSTRATED BY MARYANN FREE SMITH

BOOKCRAFT

SALT LAKE CITY, UTAH

Faith is kneeling to pray when your pet rabbit runs away faster than you can catch her.

Hope is looking and looking and looking for her.

And *charity* is hearing your Daddy choose you instead of whoever is on the telephone, "Oh, I'd like to. But not tonight. We have a lost bunny to find."

Faith is putting on your best dress and going to hear the prophet speak.

Hope is standing on your tippytoes when he comes in.

And *charity* is a lift from your big brother, helping you see the prophet walk by.

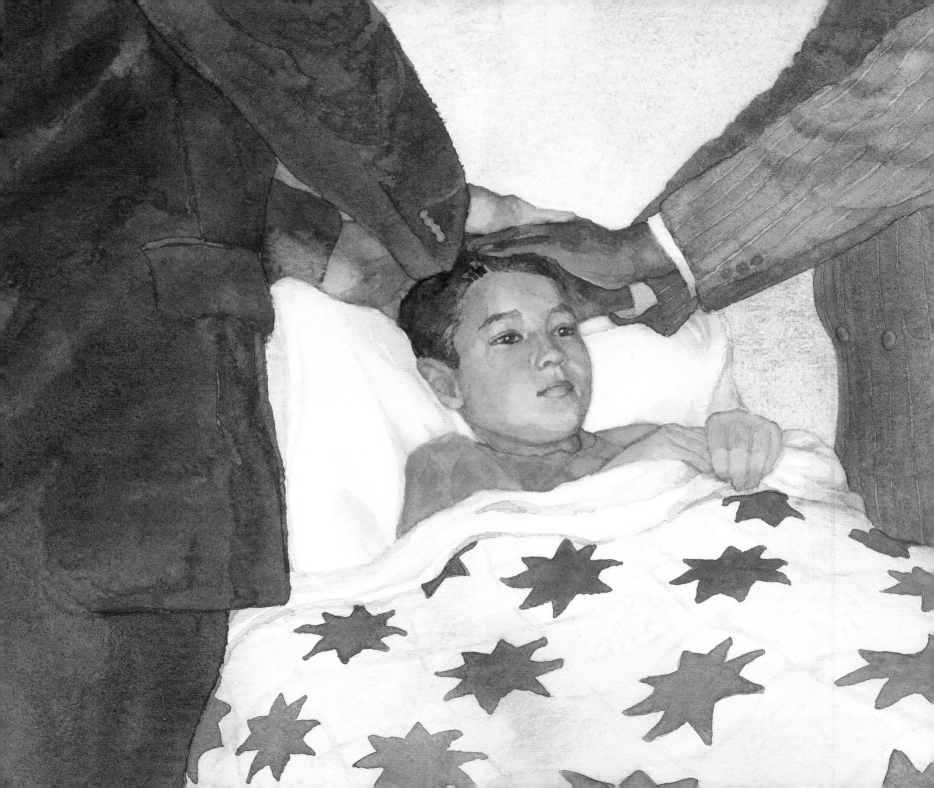

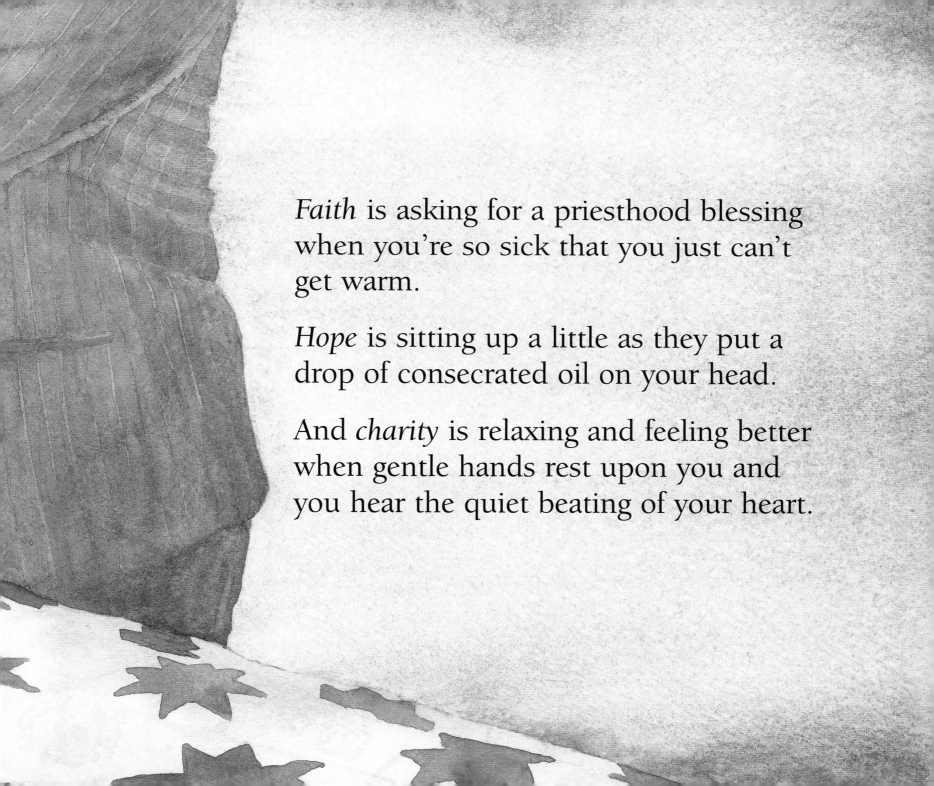

Faith is asking for a priesthood blessing when you're so sick that you just can't get warm.

Hope is sitting up a little as they put a drop of consecrated oil on your head.

And *charity* is relaxing and feeling better when gentle hands rest upon you and you hear the quiet beating of your heart.

Faith is inviting a friend to go to church with you.

Hope is watching to make sure you find seats together during Primary.

And *charity* is letting him take your favorite chair, the one by the window that everyone knows you like.

Faith is figuring how much of your birthday money is tithing.

Hope is placing the coins in an envelope that has the bishop's name on it.

And *charity* is smiling as you lick it shut, knowing that you chose the right.

Faith is deciding to get baptized by immersion—like Jesus was.

Hope is wanting the water to be warm, just like your Primary teacher said.

And *charity* is feeling so good, all dressed in white, that you forget to check.

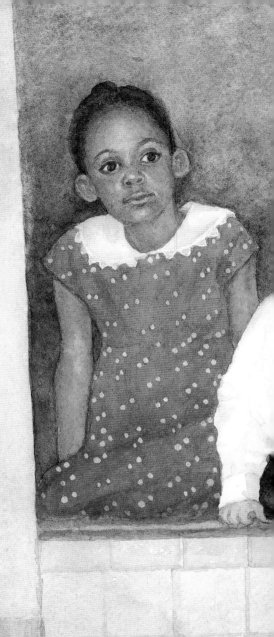

Faith is saying you're sorry after you told the whole class that your best friend's socks don't match.

Hope is trusting she'll still be your friend.

And *charity* is walking arm-in-arm with her, as if nothing ever happened.

Faith is fasting for the very first time.

Hope is noticing that lots of people who you love are fasting, too.

And *charity* is being surprised at how good you feel, two meals and no snacks later.

Faith is giving a talk all by yourself.

Hope is practicing it over and over again.

And *charity* is the peace you feel as you remember what you wanted to say.

A little while after Grandpa dies, *faith* is reminding yourself you won't always feel so sad when you see his empty chair.

Hope is imagining what Grandpa is doing now that he's in the spirit world.

And *charity* is cuddling up in the softest part of his chair, knowing you'll be together again.

Faith is turning away when someone at school tries to tell you something bad.

Hope is thinking about a Primary song, so you won't have to listen.

And *charity* is feeling better when you talk to your mom about it.

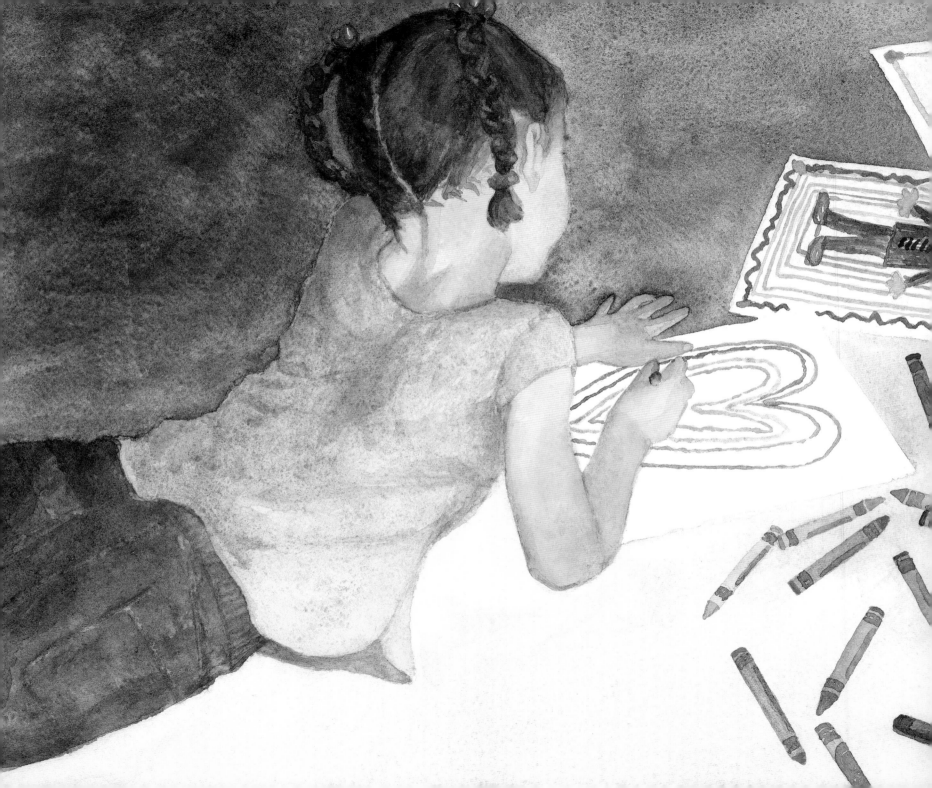

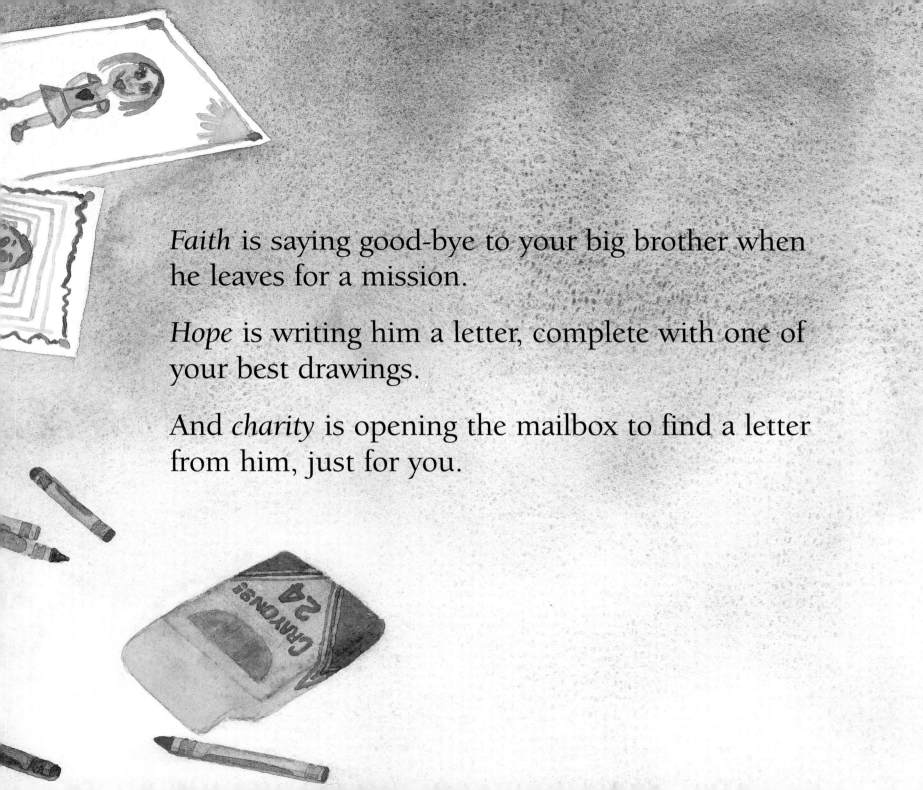

Faith is saying good-bye to your big brother when he leaves for a mission.

Hope is writing him a letter, complete with one of your best drawings.

And *charity* is opening the mailbox to find a letter from him, just for you.

Faith is loving to see the temple, even though you haven't been inside it yet.

Hope is asking your grandma what it means to have a temple recommend.

And *charity* is when she takes you on her lap, lets you hold her recommend, and says, "Families can be together forever."

Faith is sitting quietly during the sacrament.

Hope is thinking about Jesus when you eat
the bread and drink the water.

And *charity* is feeling just how
much he loves you.

"Wherefore, there must be faith; and if there must be faith
there must also be hope; and if there must be hope there must
also be charity. And except ye have charity ye can in nowise be saved
in the kingdom of God; neither can ye be saved in the kingdom of
God if ye have not faith; neither can ye if ye have no hope."

—MORONI 10:20–21